how FAST are they?

First published in 2003 by Orpheus Books Ltd.,
2 Church Green, Witney, Oxfordshire, OX28 4AW

Copyright © 2003 Orpheus Books Ltd.

Created and produced by Nicholas Harris, Claire Aston and
Emma Godfrey, Orpheus Books Ltd.

Text Nicholas Harris

Consultant Dr Charles Evans, astronomer, writer and
broadcaster

Illustrated by Sebastian Quigley *(Linden Artists)* and
Ray Grinaway

Other illustrator Mike Fuller

ISBN 1 901323 69 2

A CIP record for this book is available from the British Library.

Printed and bound in Singapore.

how FAST are they?

Orpheus

6   **8 centimetres per hour – 3.5 kilometres per hour**

Amoeba • Garden snail • Sloth • Giant tortoise • Cockroach

8   **5 – 14 kilometres per hour**

Person walking • Sprint swimmer • American woodcock • Polar bear swimming • Rat • Benz 1885 car • Crocodile running

10   **18 – 24 kilometres per hour**

Pig • Honey bee • *Santa Maria* • Marathon runner • *Tyrannosaurus rex* • Sea trout

12   **29 – 40 kilometres per hour**

Dragonfly • Female sprinter • Stagecoach • Male sprinter • African elephant • *Titanic*

14   **45 – 56 kilometres per hour**

Speed ice skater • *Rocket* • Wright *Flyer* • Rhinoceros • Tiger shark • Polar bear running • Racing yacht

16   **65 – 84 kilometres per hour**

Red kangaroo • Greyhound • Racehorse • Racing cyclist • Brown hare • Ostrich • Bluefin tuna • Thomson's gazelle • Submarine • Windsurfer

THE AMOEBA is a kind of protist. Neither plants nor animals, protists are microscopic living things, each made up of only one cell (the building block of life). An amoeba is like a plastic bag full of jelly and moves by flowing like a liquid. It can travel about eight centimetres in an hour—a fair speed for a creature itself only a fraction of a millimetre long.

A snail moves by sliding over the slime produced by its single, large foot. When it needs to, it can quickly protect itself from danger by disappearing into its shell.

**Amoeba
8 centimetres
per hour**

**Garden snail
50 metres
per hour**

0.0008 km/h

0.05 km/h

Three-toed sloth 190 metres per hour

Galápagos giant tortoise 370 metres per hour

Cockroach 3.5 km/h

Sloths spend so much of their lives in the trees, they are unable to walk normally on the ground. Instead, they hang upside down from the branches using their curved, hook-like claws to grip on. They eat, mate and give birth hanging upside down. Even their fur grows downwards. Tiny, plant-like algae grow on their coats, giving sloths a greenish tinge. Although they move extremely slowly, sloths are able to strike out quickly with their claws when threatened.

Like snails, tortoises have a shell to protect them from attack, so do not have to move very quickly at all. The Galápagos giant tortoise may live for more than 150 years.

By comparison, cockroaches are sprinters, scuttling away on their long legs whenever danger threatens.

7

0.2 km/h   1 km/h   3 km/h

A SPRINT SWIMMER can power through the water faster than you can walk—but he or she would soon be overtaken by a polar bear. Speedy over land or ice (it can easily outrun a reindeer), the polar bear is also an excellent swimmer. It needs to be, in order to cross from one floating slab of ice to the next. A polar bear can travel as fast through water as a rat can scurry about on land. The bear uses its powerful front limbs to pull its large body along through the icy water.

The American woodcock is believed to be the slowest-flying of all birds. It travels just quickly enough to keep it from falling out of the sky! It is a shy bird that feeds mainly on earthworms.

American woodcock 8 km/h

Sprint swimmer 8 km/h

Walking pace 5 km/h

5 km/h   7 km/h   8 km/h   9 km/h

The first successful car was built by German engineer Karl Benz in 1885. He fitted a petrol engine to a three-wheeled tricycle. The rear wheels were connected to the engine by belts and bicycle chains. At first, Benz's car lurched uneasily around the streets of Mannheim. But he soon perfected it. Three years later, his wife took the car on a 100-kilometre trip to visit relatives, thus becoming the first person to make a long journey by car.

A crocodile can run quite fast when it needs to. Usually, it pushes itself along on its belly, its tail whipping from side to side. Some smaller kinds of crocodile can even bound along like a rabbit!

Rat
10 km/h

Benz 1885 car
(early petrol
engine car)
13 km/h

9

Polar bear
swimming
10 km/h

THE FASTEST REPTILES

1	Pacific leatherback turtle	35 km/h
2	Spiny-tailed iguana	34.9 km/h
3	Zebra-tailed lizard	28.9 km/h
4	Six-lined racerunner	27 km/h
5	Great Basin whiptail	24.1 km/h
6	Black mamba snake	23 km/h

Crocodile running
14 km/h

10 km/h   11 km/h   12 km/h   13 km/h   14 km/h

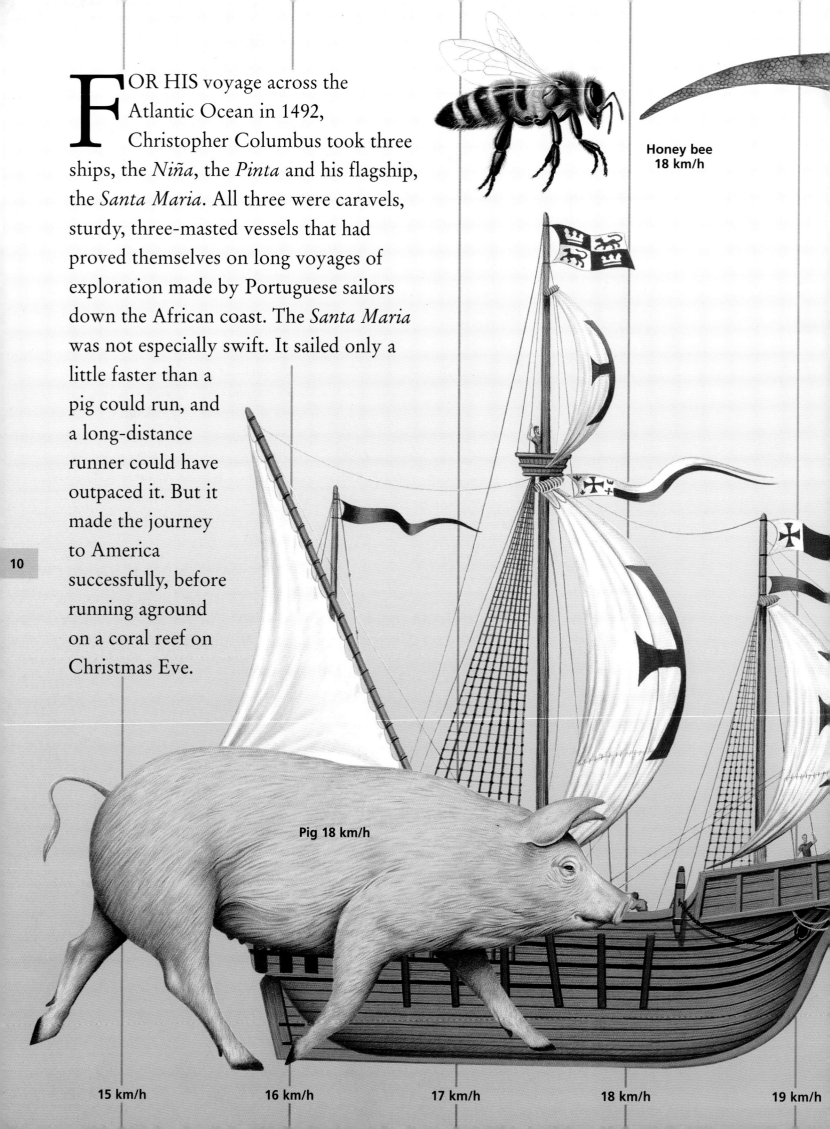

FOR HIS voyage across the Atlantic Ocean in 1492, Christopher Columbus took three ships, the *Niña*, the *Pinta* and his flagship, the *Santa Maria*. All three were caravels, sturdy, three-masted vessels that had proved themselves on long voyages of exploration made by Portuguese sailors down the African coast. The *Santa Maria* was not especially swift. It sailed only a little faster than a pig could run, and a long-distance runner could have outpaced it. But it made the journey to America successfully, before running aground on a coral reef on Christmas Eve.

Honey bee
18 km/h

Pig 18 km/h

15 km/h   16 km/h   17 km/h   18 km/h   19 km/h

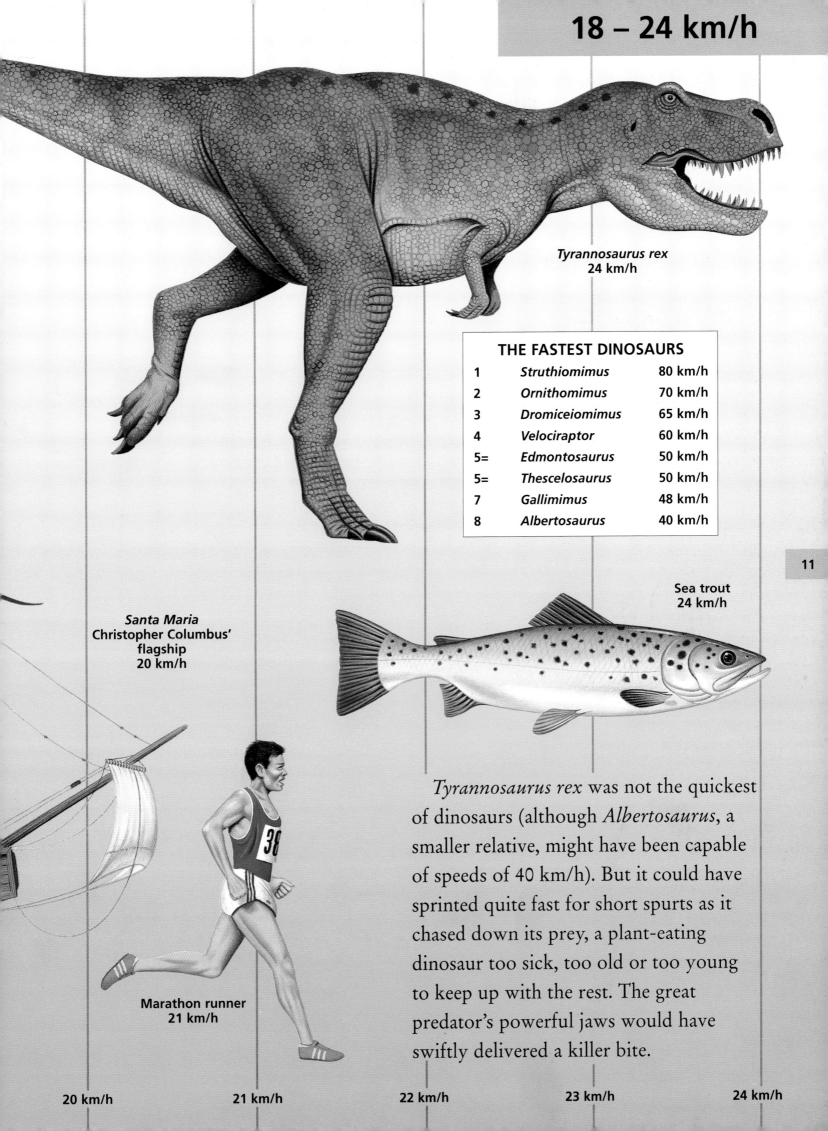

Tyrannosaurus rex
24 km/h

THE FASTEST DINOSAURS

1	*Struthiomimus*	80 km/h
2	*Ornithomimus*	70 km/h
3	*Dromiceiomimus*	65 km/h
4	*Velociraptor*	60 km/h
5=	*Edmontosaurus*	50 km/h
5=	*Thescelosaurus*	50 km/h
7	*Gallimimus*	48 km/h
8	*Albertosaurus*	40 km/h

11

Sea trout
24 km/h

Santa Maria
**Christopher Columbus'
flagship
20 km/h**

**Marathon runner
21 km/h**

Tyrannosaurus rex was not the quickest of dinosaurs (although *Albertosaurus*, a smaller relative, might have been capable of speeds of 40 km/h). But it could have sprinted quite fast for short spurts as it chased down its prey, a plant-eating dinosaur too sick, too old or too young to keep up with the rest. The great predator's powerful jaws would have swiftly delivered a killer bite.

20 km/h   **21 km/h**   **22 km/h**   **23 km/h**   **24 km/h**

**Dragonfly
29 km/h**

RUNNING AT world record pace, top male athletes can cover 100 metres in just under 10 seconds. The world's fastest women are not far behind. Both male and female sprinters could easily outpace the fastest flying insects, such as dragonflies. These creatures use their speed to dart across water and pick off other insects. They can make rapid changes of direction, including even flying backwards!

12

26 km/h   28 km/h   30 km/h   32 km/h

Over a short distance, sprinters could even keep up with a stagecoach travelling at full speed. But they would be overtaken by a stampeding African elephant. The famous ocean liner *Titanic*, which sank on its maiden voyage in 1912, steamed across the ocean at about the same speed.

Female sprinter
33 km/h

Male sprinter
36 km/h

African elephant
40 km/h

Stagecoach
34 km/h

13

Titanic ocean liner
40 km/h

34 km/h   36 km/h   38 km/h   40 km/h

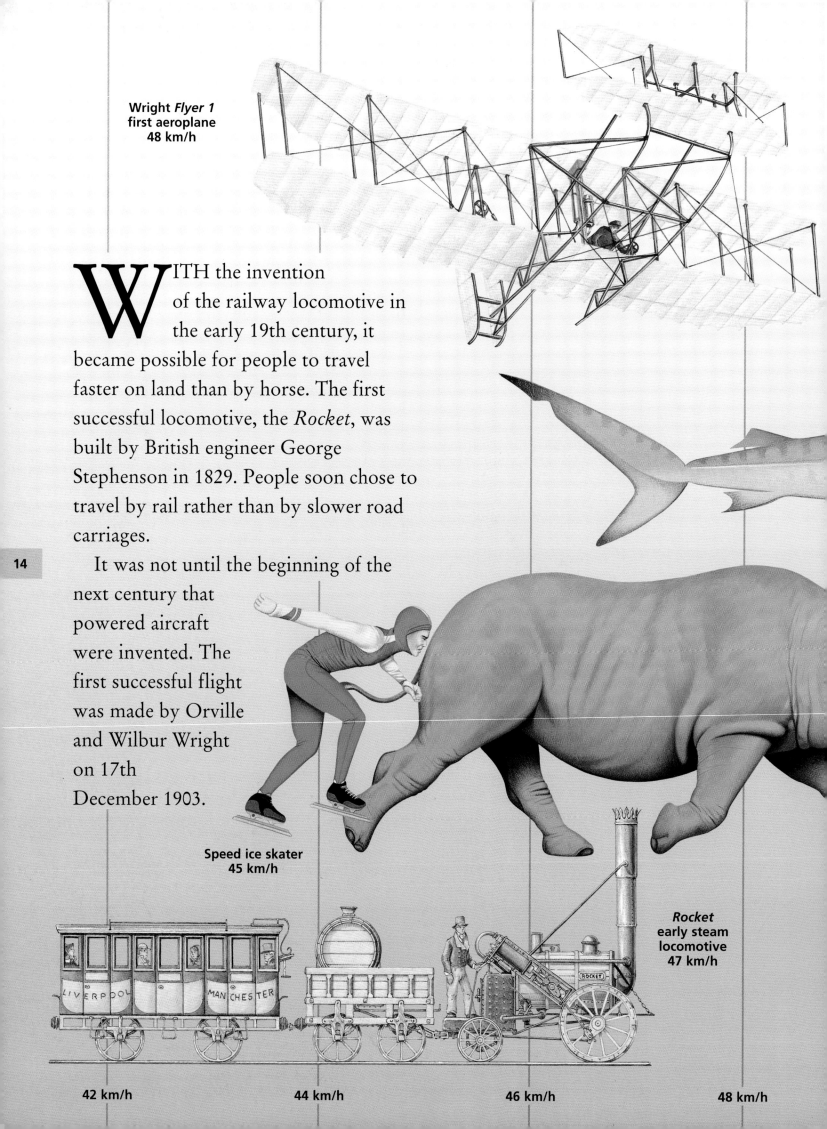

**Wright *Flyer 1*
first aeroplane
48 km/h**

W ITH the invention of the railway locomotive in the early 19th century, it became possible for people to travel faster on land than by horse. The first successful locomotive, the *Rocket*, was built by British engineer George Stephenson in 1829. People soon chose to travel by rail rather than by slower road carriages.

It was not until the beginning of the next century that powered aircraft were invented. The first successful flight was made by Orville and Wilbur Wright on 17th December 1903.

**Speed ice skater
45 km/h**

Rocket
**early steam
locomotive
47 km/h**

42 km/h   **44 km/h**   **46 km/h**   **48 km/h**

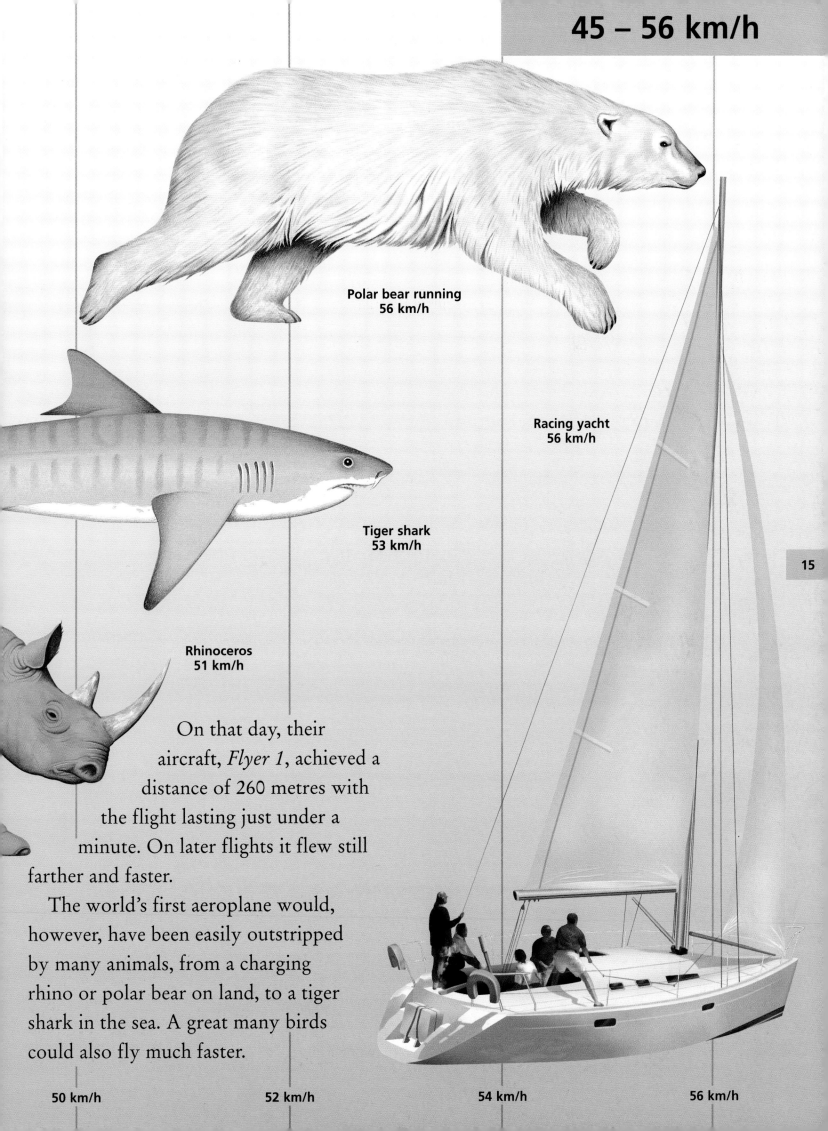

Polar bear running
56 km/h

Racing yacht
56 km/h

Tiger shark
53 km/h

Rhinoceros
51 km/h

On that day, their
aircraft, *Flyer 1*, achieved a
distance of 260 metres with
the flight lasting just under a
minute. On later flights it flew still
farther and faster.

The world's first aeroplane would,
however, have been easily outstripped
by many animals, from a charging
rhino or polar bear on land, to a tiger
shark in the sea. A great many birds
could also fly much faster.

50 km/h   52 km/h   54 km/h   56 km/h

HERE ARE SOME very fast animals, famed for their speed either around the racecourse or in the wild. To compete with them—and without the use of engine-powered vehicles—a person would have to cycle at world-record speeds, ride a champion racehorse or learn to be an extremely skilful windsurfer.

The kangaroo, hare, ostrich and gazelle are all superbly built for swift movement across open ground. The kangaroo

**Racing cyclist
71 km/h**

**Greyhound
66 km/h**

**Red kangaroo
65 km/h**

**Racehorse
69 km/h**

58 km/h   62 km/h   66 km/h   70 km/h

bounds forward on two legs. Because it needs to cover long distances quickly, this is actually a more energy-saving way of getting about than running on four legs.

The ostrich is the fastest creature on two legs. Equipped with powerful legs and supple, two-toed feet, it uses its speed to escape predators.

In the water, the streamlined tuna fish can almost keep up with one of the fastest types of submarine. It can burst forward over short distances in pursuit of its prey of fish, crustaceans and squid.

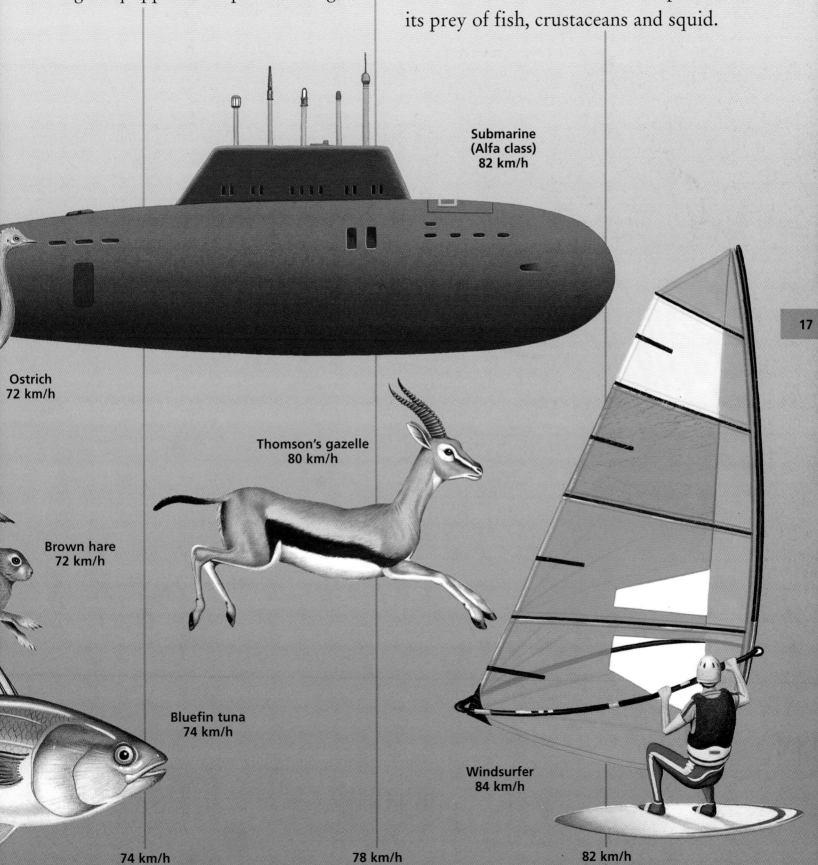

Submarine (Alfa class)
82 km/h

Ostrich
72 km/h

Thomson's gazelle
80 km/h

Brown hare
72 km/h

Bluefin tuna
74 km/h

Windsurfer
84 km/h

74 km/h   78 km/h   82 km/h

17

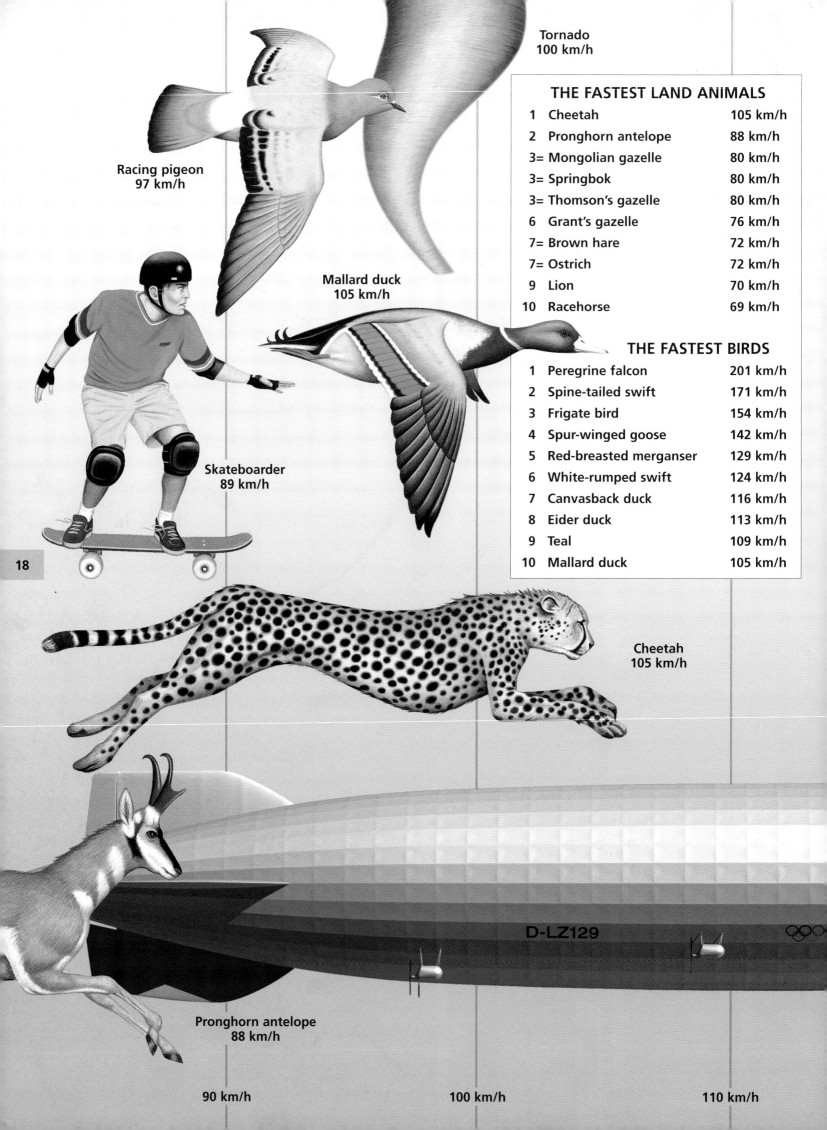

Tornado
100 km/h

Racing pigeon
97 km/h

Mallard duck
105 km/h

Skateboarder
89 km/h

Cheetah
105 km/h

Pronghorn antelope
88 km/h

D-LZ129

THE FASTEST LAND ANIMALS

1	Cheetah	105 km/h
2	Pronghorn antelope	88 km/h
3=	Mongolian gazelle	80 km/h
3=	Springbok	80 km/h
3=	Thomson's gazelle	80 km/h
6	Grant's gazelle	76 km/h
7=	Brown hare	72 km/h
7=	Ostrich	72 km/h
9	Lion	70 km/h
10	Racehorse	69 km/h

THE FASTEST BIRDS

1	Peregrine falcon	201 km/h
2	Spine-tailed swift	171 km/h
3	Frigate bird	154 km/h
4	Spur-winged goose	142 km/h
5	Red-breasted merganser	129 km/h
6	White-rumped swift	124 km/h
7	Canvasback duck	116 km/h
8	Eider duck	113 km/h
9	Teal	109 km/h
10	Mallard duck	105 km/h

90 km/h   100 km/h   110 km/h

WE HAVE now caught up with the fastest land animals—and all but the very fastest birds.

Over short bursts, the cheetah can run faster than any other animal in the world. With its long legs and lean, muscular body, it is perfectly built for speed. The cheetah uses its speed to catch its prey, including antelope, hares and young ostriches. Several adults may together chase down larger animals such as zebra. When the cheetah reaches its victim, it fells it with a bite to the throat.

Considered the fastest land animal over long distances, the pronghorn lives in North America.

It needs its speed to escape danger on the wide open grasslands that are its home. A four-day-old pronghorn is able to run faster than a man.

Tornadoes are the most powerful storms. A twisting column of air with wind speeds of more than 400 km/h, the tornado itself can cover ground at up to 100 km/h, destroying everything in its path over a journey lasting several hours.

The great airships of the 1930s measured more than 200 metres in length. At their top speed of about 130 km/h, they could travel faster than most birds. But they would be outpaced by an Olympic luge champion, riding a tiny sled flat on his or her back less than eight centimetres above the ice.

Luge
137 km/h

Hindenburg airship
130 km/h

19

120 km/h

130 km/h

140 km/h

Spine-tailed swift
171 km/h

THE PEREGRINE FALCON is considered to be the fastest-moving living thing. In a steep dive to catch other birds in mid-flight (known as "stooping"), it may top 200 km/h. In level flight, however, the spine-tailed swift is probably the fastest bird. Superbly streamlined, it swoops through the air catching insects in its gaping beak.

Peregrine falcon
201 km/h

Table tennis smash
170 km/h

MALLARD

Mallard
steam locomotive
201 km/h

160 km/h   180 km/h   200 km/h

Tennis serve
240 km/h

Light aircraft
262 km/h

Downhill
skier
241 km/h

Powerboat
250 km/h

WATER SPEED RECORD

8 Oct 1978   Ken Warby (Aus)
Spirit of Australia   511.11 km/h

20 Nov 1977   Ken Warby (Aus)
Spirit of Australia   464.44 km/h

30 June 1967   Lee A Taylor (US)
Hustler   458.99 km/h

31 Dec 1964 Donald Campbell (UK)
Bluebird K7   444.70 km/h

14 May 1959 Donald Campbell (UK)
Bluebird K7   418.98 km/h

10 Nov 1958 Donald Campbell (UK)
Bluebird K7   400.10 km/h

In 1938 the steam locomotive *Mallard* set a record over a distance of 400 metres that stands to this day. It was fitted with a special streamlined casing.

The water speed record is held by the *Spirit of Australia* (see page 23). The top speed of most powerboats is about half that. High-speed travel must overcome friction caused by the roughness of the water's surface. This is much less of a problem when moving on ice or through the air.

220 km/h   240 km/h   260 km/h

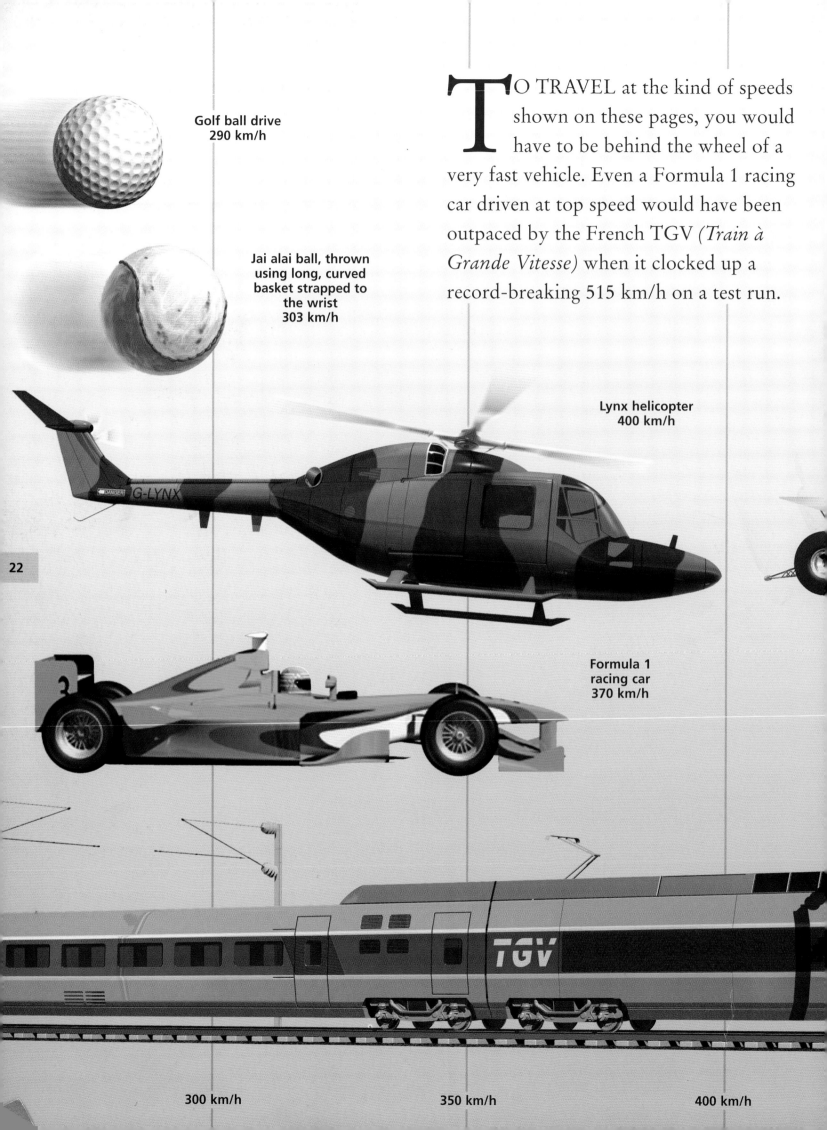

Golf ball drive
290 km/h

Jai alai ball, thrown using long, curved basket strapped to the wrist
303 km/h

T O TRAVEL at the kind of speeds shown on these pages, you would have to be behind the wheel of a very fast vehicle. Even a Formula 1 racing car driven at top speed would have been outpaced by the French TGV *(Train à Grande Vitesse)* when it clocked up a record-breaking 515 km/h on a test run.

Lynx helicopter
400 km/h

G-LYNX

Formula 1 racing car
370 km/h

TGV

300 km/h   **350 km/h**   **400 km/h**

Helicopters are better known for their manoeuvrability and for vertical take-off and landing capability rather than for speed. But the racing car could not keep up with a Lynx flying at full throttle. The helicopter would itself be overtaken by a dragster (a car built for acceleration contests), the current holder of the water speed record, the *Spirit of Australia*, and the world's fastest motorcycle.

All these speedy extreme machines would, however, be beaten for speed by an arrow fired from a longbow using just human muscle power!

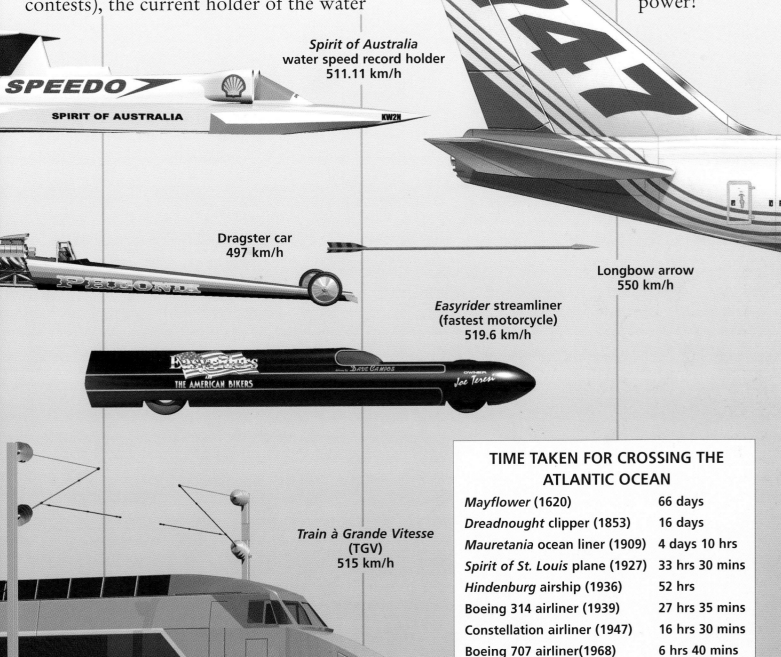

Spirit of Australia
water speed record holder
511.11 km/h

SPEEDO
SPIRIT OF AUSTRALIA
KW2N

Dragster car
497 km/h

Longbow arrow
550 km/h

Easyrider streamliner
(fastest motorcycle)
519.6 km/h

THE AMERICAN BIKERS

Train à Grande Vitesse
(TGV)
515 km/h

SNCF

TIME TAKEN FOR CROSSING THE ATLANTIC OCEAN

Mayflower (1620)	66 days
Dreadnought clipper (1853)	16 days
Mauretania ocean liner (1909)	4 days 10 hrs
Spirit of St. Louis plane (1927)	33 hrs 30 mins
Hindenburg airship (1936)	52 hrs
Boeing 314 airliner (1939)	27 hrs 35 mins
Constellation airliner (1947)	16 hrs 30 mins
Boeing 707 airliner(1968)	6 hrs 40 mins
Concorde (1974)	2 hrs 56 mins
Lockheed SR-71 (1974)	1 hr 55 mins

23

450 km/h   500 km/h   550 km/h

BOEING 747-400

Boeing 747
(Jumbo Jet)
978 km/h

Bell X-1
Glamorous Glennis
1127 km/h

Revolver bullet
933 km/h

ThrustSSC
land speed record holder
1227.723 km/h

24

600 km/h

1000 km/h

ON THIS DOUBLE PAGE, we pass the speed of sound: about 1225 km/h at sea level, or Mach 1. All forms of transport that go faster than the speed of sound (or "break the sound barrier") are called supersonic. The first aircraft to fly at supersonic speeds was the Bell X-1, piloted by US pilot Chuck Yeager on 14 October 1947. Named *Glamorous Glennis* after Yeager's wife, it actually reached a speed of 1127 km/h , but the speed of sound is lower at high altitudes. Most modern fighter aircraft, such as the F-16, can fly much faster than Mach 1.

The first supersonic airliner, the Russian Tupolev-144, flew in 1968. But Concorde is the only supersonic airliner flying today. Cruising at 18,000 metres, it flies at more than twice the speed of sound (Mach 2). Other airliners, such as the Boeing 747, are "subsonic".

It was not until 1997 that the a land vehicle broke the sound barrier officially for the first time. *ThrustSSC*, driven by Andy Green, had two huge jet engines.

F-16
modern fighter aircraft
2452 km/h

Concorde
supersonic airliner
2333 km/h

1500 km/h   2000 km/h   2500 km/h

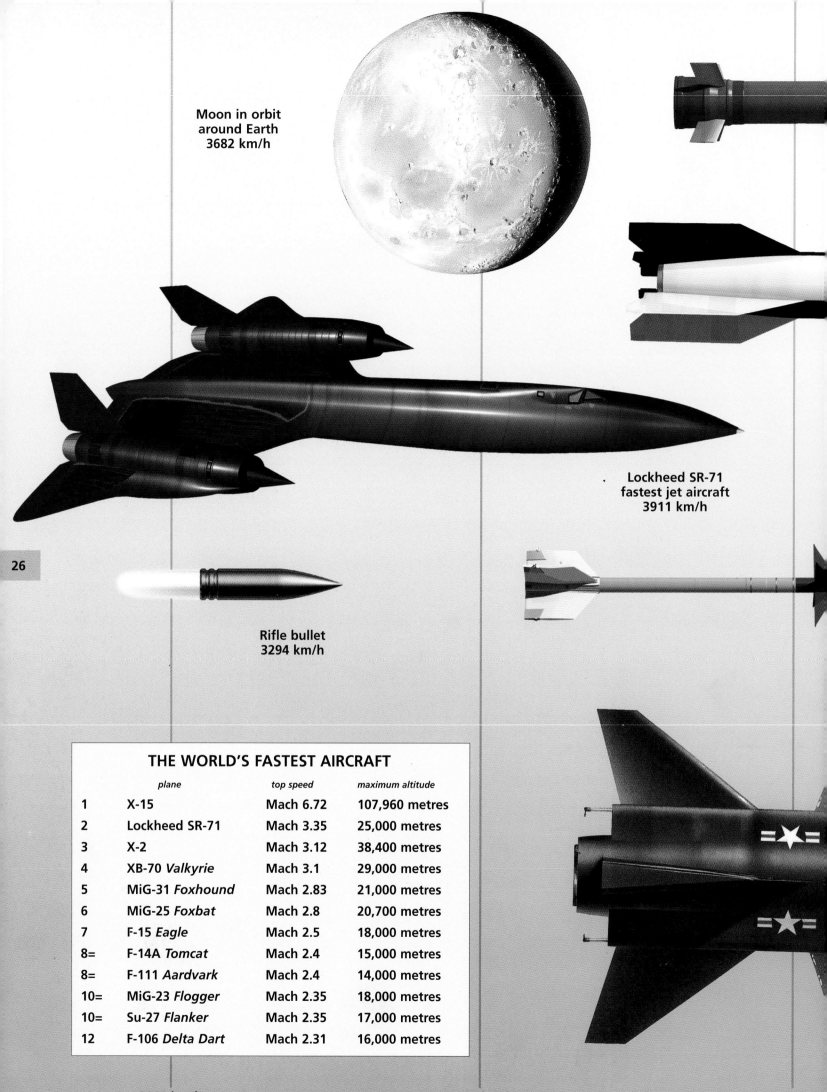

Moon in orbit
around Earth
3682 km/h

Lockheed SR-71
fastest jet aircraft
3911 km/h

Rifle bullet
3294 km/h

THE WORLD'S FASTEST AIRCRAFT

	plane	top speed	maximum altitude
1	X-15	Mach 6.72	107,960 metres
2	Lockheed SR-71	Mach 3.35	25,000 metres
3	X-2	Mach 3.12	38,400 metres
4	XB-70 *Valkyrie*	Mach 3.1	29,000 metres
5	MiG-31 *Foxhound*	Mach 2.83	21,000 metres
6	MiG-25 *Foxbat*	Mach 2.8	20,700 metres
7	F-15 *Eagle*	Mach 2.5	18,000 metres
8=	F-14A *Tomcat*	Mach 2.4	15,000 metres
8=	F-111 *Aardvark*	Mach 2.4	14,000 metres
10=	MiG-23 *Flogger*	Mach 2.35	18,000 metres
10=	Su-27 *Flanker*	Mach 2.35	17,000 metres
12	F-106 *Delta Dart*	Mach 2.31	16,000 metres

3000 km/h   3500 km/h   4000 km/h

Anti-tank
projectile
4388 km/h

V2
World War II
long-range rocket
4828 km/h

Sidewinder
surface-to-air
missile
4186 km/h

W E HAVE NOW reached the realm of extreme speed: aircraft, rockets and missiles that can overtake a rifle bullet—and even travel faster than the Moon in its orbit around the Earth.

Although more than 30 years old, the US spyplane Lockheed SR-71 is still the world's fastest jet aircraft. Flying at an altitude of 25,000 metres, it can easily go faster than Mach 3 (three times the speed of sound). At such high speeds, its surface—coated with heat-radiating paint—reaches 300°C. The aircraft itself grows nearly 80 centimetres longer!

The fastest aircraft of all is the American experimental plane, the X-15. It is carried aloft attached to the underside of a transporter plane, from where its rocket engines blast it off into the sky. Not only is the X-15 the first aircraft to go faster than Mach 4, 5 and 6, it also holds the altitude record of 107,960 metres—on the edge of space itself.

27

X-15
fastest
aircraft
7274 km/h

4500 km/h   5000 km/h   6000 km/h   7000 km/h   8000 km/h

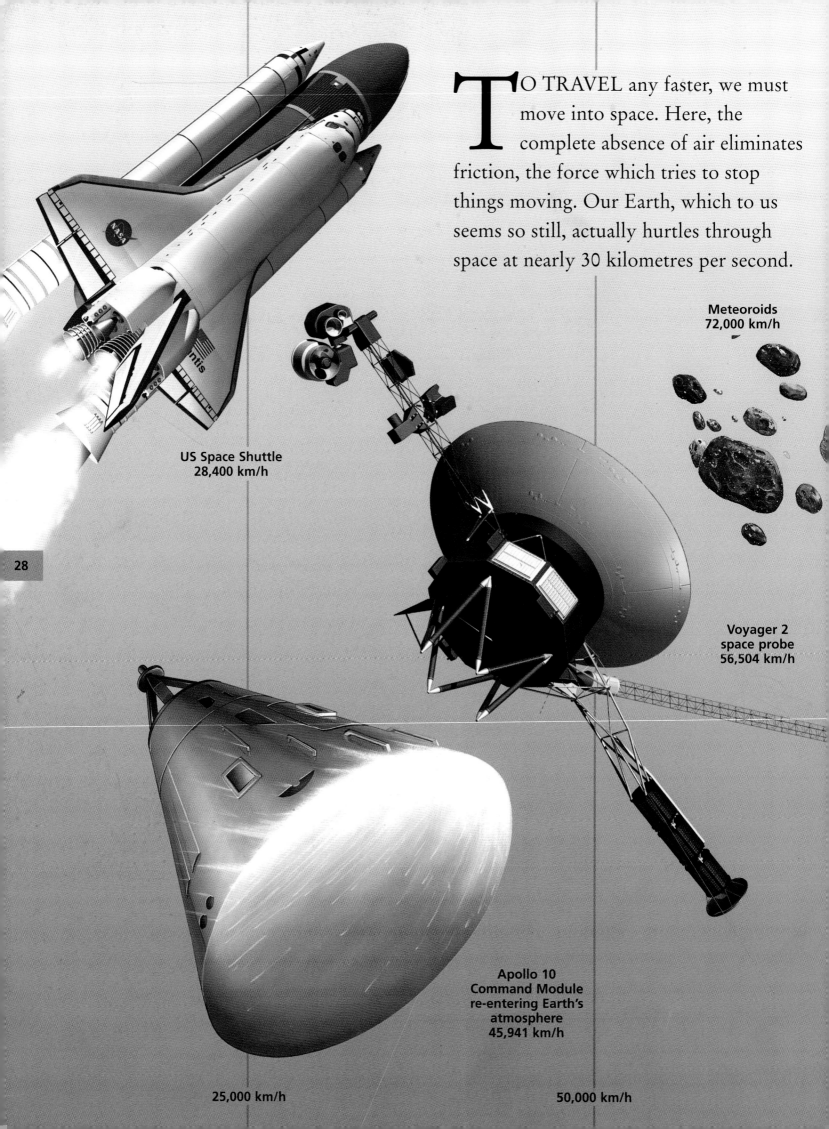

To TRAVEL any faster, we must move into space. Here, the complete absence of air eliminates friction, the force which tries to stop things moving. Our Earth, which to us seems so still, actually hurtles through space at nearly 30 kilometres per second.

Meteoroids
72,000 km/h

US Space Shuttle
28,400 km/h

Voyager 2
space probe
56,504 km/h

Apollo 10
Command Module
re-entering Earth's
atmosphere
45,941 km/h

25,000 km/h   50,000 km/h

It is not the fastest planet, however. That record goes to Mercury, the nearest planet to the Sun. It completes its orbit around the Sun in just 88 days.

Meteoroids, small lumps of rock that were once part of asteroids, zip around space faster than the fastest man-made object, the space probe Voyager 2. This unmanned spacecraft, which was launched in 1977 on a journey to fly close by the giant planets, Jupiter, Saturn, Uranus and Neptune, and take detailed photographs of them, has since left the Solar System. It still sends back signals to Earth from many billions of kilometres away!

To travel into space, a vehicle must overcome the Earth's gravity. It has to travel at a speed of at least 28,400 km/h—what is sometimes called escape velocity—in order to be able to do this. Only modern rockets, such as those used on the Space Shuttle, have sufficient power.

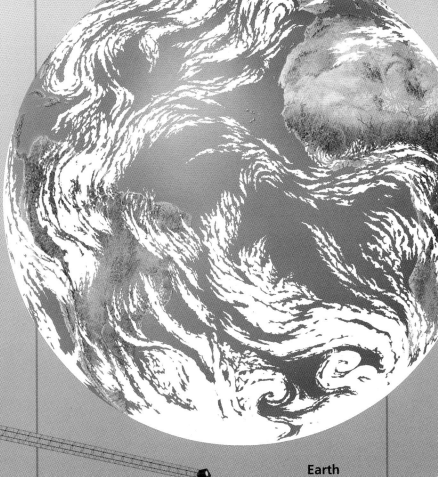

Earth
107,226 km/h

Mercury
172,440 km/h

HOW FAST ARE THE PLANETS?		
1	Mercury	48 km per second
2	Venus	35 km per second
3	Earth	30 km per second
4	Mars	24 km per second
5	Jupiter	13 km per second
6	Saturn	10 km per second
7	Uranus	7 km per second
8	Neptune	5.5 km per second
9	Pluto	4.5 km per second

75,000 km/h

100,000 km/h